Pages 2 and 3:
Photo by
Harry V. Lacey

Pages 34 and 35:
Photo courtesy of
Vogelpark Walsrode

t.f.h.
Your First
FINCH

George W. Noreen

Introduction

The finches are ideal birds for the home: they are small, quiet and colorful, and bring a hint of the tropical and the exotic into our lives. Most finches can be easily accommodated in the ordinary all-wire cages available at petshops and retail outlets. The larger the cage the better, however, and the most practical type is the so-called breeding or large stock cage, which is rectangular in shape. Actually, many of the smaller species of finch do best in box cages, i.e., a solid box with only one side wired.

All cages must, of course, allow for easy cleaning, watering and feeding, as well as the installation of perches. Perches are best made from natural tree branches of varying thickness and should not be placed over food or water receptacles. Natural perches are readily procured, can easily be replaced when dirty, and are much the best for keeping the bird's feet healthy.

Outdoor aviaries are the ideal method of housing most finch species, and they are necessary for good breeding results from many of them, especially the more insectivorous forms such as waxbills. Do not, however, let this fact deter you from obtaining and keeping an interesting collection of finches in indoor cages.

FEEDING

All of the finches discussed in this text are quite easily fed on a diet of seeds, greens, and insectivore mixture. The favorite type of seed varies somewhat with the species of bird, but all should be offered a wide variety.

Most important of the seeds to the majority of finches are the millets. As an example, the diet of the waxbills consists of about 80% small yellow millet, 10% large white millet, and 10% canary seed.

The small grassfinches show nearly the same preference, but the larger birds, such as Shaft-tails, consume a slightly larger percentage of large white millet and canary seed. The mannikins also show a greater desire for the white millet, although like the others, they consume more of the small yellow millet than any other seeds. Their seed intake averages to about 60% small yellow millet, 30% large white millet, and 10% canary seed.

From these figures it can be seen that the most important seed for the majority of these birds is the small yellow millet usually sold under the name finch millet. This is the same seed that comes in spray form, which is most important to the diet of certain species, such as Gouldian Finches.

Seeds may be conveniently fed

by purchasing the regular packaged "finch" mixtures commonly available, but care must be taken to see that these mixtures contain the proper ingredients. If not they may be supplemented by separate seeds. The large millet (*Panicum miliaceum*) is called "proso" or "hog" millet by many dealers, while the small yellow millet (*Setaria italica*) is often called "Italian" or "foxtail" millet. Canary seed (*Phalaris canariensis*) is most often called just that, and it is commonly imported.

Another small form of millet that is sometimes available is known as "Japanese" or "barnyard" millet (*Echinochloa crusgalli*), and it is also a good addition to the diet of these birds.

In practice it is probably best to feed all the different kinds of seed separately, but since this requires too many food containers it is usually easier to make up a mixture of seeds to place in one dish or food cup. By using the foregoing seed preference percentage figures it is possible to arrive at a good overall mixture for the birds included here.

A standard mixture for small finches might read as follows: four parts small yellow (finch) millet; one-half part large white (proso) millet; one-half part canary seed.

A standard mixture for large finches might look like this: three parts small yellow (finch) millet; one and one-half parts large white or (proso) millet; one and one-half part canary seed.

These seeds are especially beneficial when fed in sprouted form. They may be sprouted by soaking them in water for a few hours and then spreading them on a damp cloth that is then put in a warm place until the seeds sprout.

The true finches, of course, require an even greater variety of seed in their diet, and it is well to purchase one of the many wild grass seed mixtures, available from most petshops, to use in conjunction with the mixtures listed above.

A variety of greens should also be offered. Among the best are leaf lettuce, chickweed, spinach, dandelion, and carrot tops, to name a few.

Other foods that may be given from time to time include crumbled boiled (at least 25 minutes) egg yolk, soaked ant eggs, milk-soaked whole wheat bread (not too sloppy), and insectivore or "mocking bird" food.

A much appreciated treat can be provided by placing a clump of sod in any cage or aviary that lacks a natural earth floor. The birds find much valuable food in the form of insects and tender grass shoots and also benefit from consuming some of the dirt.

Facing page: Pair of Zebra Finches. Natural tree branches are commonly recommended perches for birds. Photo by T. Tilford. Above: The Ribbon Finch, *Amadina fasciata*, also known as the Cut-throat Finch. Photo by R. and V. Moat.

Health

Birds that are properly housed, fed, and otherwise attended seldom become ill. There are times, however, when diseases or other ailments occur in the best managed collections. The greatest drawback to treating sick birds (especially these small finches) is the fact that their troubles often do not manifest themselves until it is too late to do anything. It is, therefore, wise to keep a sharp lookout for signs of trouble, which are sometimes difficult to detect. But when a bird sits ruffled up with its head under its wing and both feet on the perch, something is likely to be wrong.

The most important and useful treatment for many (in fact most) bird ailments is heat. This is best applied within the bounds of a hospital cage, which is fully enclosed with glass on the front and has means of maintaining a constant temperature of from 85 to 90°F. This cage should also have provisions for feeding, watering and cleaning.

When in use, this cage should be kept at a temperature of at least 85°F for about the first 24 hours, after which the heat can be lowered gradually by about 5°F each succeeding 24-hour period. This heat treatment often works wonders, and it is especially useful in cases of chills, egg-binding, and many obscure ailments.

Antibiotics are also of great value in treating many illnesses common to finches. Some of them are available in tablet form at petshops, but they must be used only as instructed—it is strongly advised that you give your bird(s) only medications that have been prescribed by your veterinarian.

Newly received birds should be quarantined and kept apart from others for a period of at least two weeks. They should also be treated with a parasite-killing spray or powder to eliminate any lice or mites they may be carrying.

When first released from the shipping crate, the finch should not be poked out, nor shaken out, but allowed to emerge at its leisure after the box or crate has been placed in or near the cage or aviary. It is also wise to release the birds into their new home early in the day if possible.

KEEPING THE NAILS TRIM
It will occasionally be necessary to trim the toe nails of some of these birds, especially those of certain nuns or mannikins. This simple operation may be performed with a pair of regular nail clippers or small scissors. To prevent bleeding, care must be taken not to cut into the quick, the vein that runs into the claw. The quick can be noted by holding the nail up to a strong light.

True Finches

Some of the birds found in the family of true finches, Fringillidae, are among the most popular of all cage and aviary birds. This is the family to which the common canary belongs, and like it, the following birds are primarily seed eaters. Most also feed on insects and fruit and vegetable matter to varying degrees. All require grit or fine gravel for digestive purposes and must be constantly supplied with water for drinking and bathing. Finches should also have some form of lime-containing material, such as cuttlebone or baked and finely ground egg shell, available to them at all times as a help in their producing good hard-shelled eggs.

The sexes in many species differ in appearance, but some are alike and can be sexed only by the behavior or the song of the male. With only few exceptions, finches build open cup-shaped nests, and it is usually the female who does all the nest building and incubation, which lasts 12 to 14 days. Young finches are at first fed by regurgitation from the crop of both parents and leave the nest after about 14 or 15 days.

Most finches are quite hardy in respect to temperature, but some, e.g., Rainbow Bunting, cannot tolerate too much cold.

The majority of finches do not bother other birds except during the breeding season, although the larger species cannot be trusted with smaller birds.

RAINBOW BUNTING

The Orange-breasted or Rainbow Bunting (*Passerina leclancherii*) comes from western Mexico and is one of the most beautiful of all finches. The male is turquoise blue on the back and wings with apple-green on the crown of the head; his breast is orange, shading to yellow on the belly and underparts. The female is not so brightly colored but mainly olive green with a trace of blue above and yellow below. Length, about five inches.

This colorful little finch has been bred in captivity on only a few occasions. It is fond of mealworms, which must be strictly rationed when fed (about four or five per day). The diet should contain canary, millets, and wild grass seeds along with plenty of insectivore mixture.

Rainbow Buntings are somewhat delicate when first imported into more temperate climates and require controlled temperatures; but they soon become quite hardy.

Above: Chestnut-flanked White Zebra Finch. There are many color varieties of the Zebra Finch but they are all considered to be of the species *Poephila guttata*. Photo by R. and V. Moat. Facing page: Diamond Sparrow, *E mblema guttata*, also known as the Diamond Firetail. Photo by M. Gilroy.

CUBAN MELODIOUS FINCH

Perhaps best known of the small West Indian finches known as "grass-quits" is the Cuban Melodious Finch (*Tiaris canora*). The male is yellowish green above; a black mask covers the face and is encircled by a broad yellow collar; the breast is black, shading into gray on the sides and abdomen. The female resembles the male but has the black of the face replaced with chestnut, and the yellow collar is smaller and duller in color. Length, about four and one-half inches.

Unlike others of its family, this bird builds a spherical covered nest and often will, in captivity, make use of a nest box. The eggs are white, sometimes spotted with reddish-brown, and both sexes incubate. Young birds should be separated from their parents as soon as they are able to fend for themselves, or they are likely to be attacked and killed. Males are very pugnacious at all times towards others of their kind but are quite safe in mixed collections.

The diet for this species may contain canary, millet, and wild grass seeds along with insectivore mixture, greens, etc.

EUROPEAN GOLDFINCH

The European Goldfinch (*Carduelis carduelis*) is a popular and well-known cage and aviary bird. It is often used for crossing with canary hens to obtain the singing "mules" which are popular in Europe.

The face is red, with a thin black line around the eyes and bill. The crown and a band descending down each side of the neck are black. The sides of the head and neck are white. Back, breast, and flanks are cinnamon-brown. The wings black, with a broad transverse band of yellow, and white feather tips. The tail is black, with the inner webs tipped white. Belly, underparts, under and upper tail coverts, white. Bill, whitish. The female is very similar but duller in color. Length about five and one-half inches.

The open cup-shaped nest of this species is built of grass and roots mixed with down and, in captivity, will readily be placed into an open box or other cup-like receptacle. A clutch consists of four or five pale blue eggs which are speckled with brown. The hen alone incubates, and typically two broods are reared per season.

Food for this species may consist of a variety of seeds, including canary, millets, rape, niger, etc., along with fruit, lettuce or other greens, mealworms, insectivore mixture, etc. For a small bird, this species is very long-lived—individuals having been known to live as long as 27 years.

Special Finches

The most colorful and interesting of all small seed-eating cage birds are found in the family Estrildidae, which includes 107 true species inhabiting Africa, Asia, and Australasia. They are closely related to the true finches but differ in nesting habits—most of them building globular nests with side entrances that are entered by means of a spout. Additionally some have a "cock's nest" added to the top of the structure in which the male sleeps alone. In captivity many of them will accept partly open boxes or other receptacles in which to construct their nests. Some are quite easily bred.

The eggs are white in color, and incubation lasts for a period of 11 to 14 days. The males often share in this task. The nestlings show luminous and brightly colored swollen bands or spots at the gape, and dark spots or lines on the palate or the tongue or both, which are believed to be an aid to feeding in the darkness of the nest interior. Live insect food is required for rearing the young of many species. Young birds leave the nest after about 18 to 21 days and are usually independent when about one month old. Their plumage appears different than either parent at first but matures by the close of the first year.

Most of these little birds are quite hardy, but they should be supplied with plenty of heat when first imported and are best never kept in temperatures below 50 to 55°F. They can withstand lower temperatures but will do better if kept warm.

The majority of them are peaceful and get along well in mixed groups, but individuals vary and every collection must be watched for fights and for bullying.

None of these birds should be overcrowded in small quarters as they are prone to feather picking and will soon be bald and near nude. Their diet should consist of canary, millet, and wild grass seeds along with insectivore mixture, live insects, green food and fruit. Cuttlebone, grit and water for drinking and bathing are also necessary.

The smallest members of the family are known as "waxbills" from the red sealing-wax appearance of their bills. They are found mainly in Africa, although two species come from Asia and one is native to Australia. They travel in large flocks which often consist of several species, and their spherical nests are often built in colonies. Most of the cocks have a nuptial dance during which they hold a blade of grass in the bill which is later offered to the hen. Very few of the waxbills are what could be called easy to breed but some do so quite readily if properly cared for. They feed their

Above: Cordonbleu Waxbill, *Estrilda angolensis*. The author considers this native African bird to be the most beautiful of all the waxbills. Photo by R. and V. Moat. Facing page: The Diamond Sparrow, *Emblema guttata*, a native Australian bird that has proven relatively easy to keep but rather difficult to breed in captivity. Photo by M. Gilroy.

young on insect food and success in breeding will only be achieved if plenty of live insects (tiny mealworms, fruit flies, etc.) can be supplied in addition to a good egg nestling food and insectivore mixture.

Most waxbills have sweet, high-pitched songs; some, such as the Strawberry Finches, are especially gifted in this respect.

RED-BILLED FIREFINCH

The Red-billed Firefinch (*Lagonosticta senegala*) comes from West Africa. It is almost entirely pinkish red in color, fading to yellowish brown underneath, and with brown wings and tail. The sides are spotted with tiny white spots. Bill, red; legs and feet, dark flesh color. Length, 3.5 inches. The female is light brown, fading to whitish on the underparts.

This bird becomes tamer and more friendly than most waxbills and is quite hardy when acclimatized. It breeds freely, and the young are not too difficult to rear. During the breeding season the cocks will fight, and it is best to keep only one pair in an enclosure. They do not bother other birds.

The newly fledged young resemble the female in color and show no red. Their bills are gray. Young cocks usually begin to show some red coloring when about six weeks of age.

LAVENDER FINCH

The Lavender Finch (*Estrilda coerulescens*) comes from western and southern Africa. It is a delicate blue-gray, paler on the cheeks, and darkening toward the vent. A few white spots appear on the flanks and a black streak extends through the eye. The tail, rump, upper and under caudal feathers are deep crimson. Bill, black with lateral red streak. Legs and feet, black. Length, 4 inches. Sexes alike, although the feathers around the vent are usually somewhat lighter in color on the female.

This species is somewhat delicate in captivity and is not often bred. The cocks are quite pugnacious toward each other and fight savagely, so it is best to keep only pairs in a collection. They are also among the worst of the "feather pluckers" and will not stand crowded conditions without ending up miserable and ragged in appearance.

CORDONBLEU WAXBILL

One of the most beautiful of the waxbills is the Cordonbleu Waxbill (*Estrilda angolensis*), which ranges throughout tropical Africa in several races. The male has the upper parts brown; the face, breast and sides, bright blue. The abdomen and underparts are white-brown. Tail, dark blue. Bill, red. Legs and feet, flesh colored. Length 4.5 inches. The female resembles the male but is slightly duller in color.

This bird is quite hardy in captivity and is a very free breeder, but it is not commonly imported. Dealers sometimes list it as the Blue-breasted Waxbill.

CRIMSON-EARED CORDONBLEU WAXBILL

The sub-species known as the Crimson-eared Cordonbleu Waxbill (*Estrilda angolensis bengala*), in which the male has bright red cheek patches, is the best known form of the species *E. angolensis*. It is slightly more delicate than the nominate Cordonbleu Waxbill, but if kept fairly warm and fed properly (live insects and insectivore mixture in addition to seeds), it will live well and breed quite freely. The nest of this form should never be disturbed or looked into or the birds will desert it. Young birds resemble the female and cocks do not acquire the red cheek patches until about five months of age. Like the Firefinch this bird is quite steady and becomes fairly tame in captivity.

GRAY WAXBILL

The Gray Waxbill (*Estrilda troglodytes*) comes from West Africa and is the most commonly imported of all this group. It is grayish brown above, paler on the head. The underparts are grayish white with a pink patch on the abdomen. A streak of coral red extends from the base of the beak back through the eye. Tail, dark brown. Beak, red. Legs and feet, flesh-brown. The sexes are alike, although the female often shows less pink on the underparts. Length, 4 inches.

This species is very difficult to breed in captivity, although the feat has been accomplished. It is one of the waxbills that constructs a "cock's nest" on top of the nest proper.

Dealers often list the species as the Common or Red-eared Waxbill.

ORANGE-CHEEKED WAXBILL

The Orange-cheeked Waxbill (*Estrilda melpoda*) is from western and eastern Africa. The head is light gray with bright orange cheeks; the back and wings, grayish brown; and the underparts, whitish. The rump is bright red; and the tail, blackish brown. Bill, red; legs and feet, light brown. Length, 3.5 inches. The female is like the male but not quite so bright in color and with smaller orange cheek patches.

This is a fairly hardy waxbill but nervous and a shy breeder. Young birds are similar to the adults except for the orange ear patches which are smaller and paler in color. Their bill is black.

STRAWBERRY FINCH

Most popular of all waxbills is perhaps the Strawberry Finch or Red Avadavat (*Estrilda amandava*) which ranges from India through southern Asia and Malaysia. This is the only waxbill in which the male follows the example of the weavers and the whydahs and goes out of color for part of the year. When in breeding plumage he has the upper parts of the head, back and wings deep brown. The sides of the head, throat and underparts, scarlet. The flanks, wings and under tail coverts are spotted with white and the rump is bright red. Bill, red; legs and feet, pinkish. Length, 4 inches. The

Above: Pair of Gouldian Finches, *Chloebia gouldiae*; one is of the red-headed and the other of the black-headed variety. The author feels that the Gouldian Finch is the most beautifully colored of the grassfinches. Facing page: The Zebra Finch is certainly among the most commonly kept of the grassfinches, and it breeds relatively well in indoor captivity. Photo by M. DeFreitas.

Wire finch frame.

female is brown above, with darker wings, and yellow-buff below. Her rump and upper tail coverts are dark red, and she has a few white spots on the wings. The male resembles her when out of color.

There are two forms of this bird available. The larger, and more common one is that described above which comes from India and is usually listed as the Bombay Avadavat or Tiger Finch. A smaller and usually more expensive form (*Estrilda amandava punicea*) comes from Indo-China and Java and is known as the Chinese Avadavat. It is brighter red in color and has a black abdomen.

This bird breeds readily, and the male is one of the waxbills with a real song. The plumage change is often a slow process and some individuals become quite dark, almost black, in color after a few molts in captivity.

ORANGE-BREASTED WAXBILL

Smallest of all these birds is the Orange-breasted Waxbill (*Estrilda subflava*) from West Africa. It is olive-brown above with the throat, abdomen and under tail coverts golden yellow. The breast is bright orange, and a bright red streak passes over the eye. Bill, red; legs and feet flesh color. Length, 3 inches. The female lacks the crimson eyebrow and her breast is not orange but pale yellow.

This tiny waxbill is quite hardy and breeds freely. It is one of the smallest of all finches and must be kept in cages or aviaries with very closely spaced bars. Some individuals seem to have a tendency to turn very dark in color, sometimes almost black, after being in confinement for a while. Young birds are grayish brown in color with darker wings. Their bills are black.

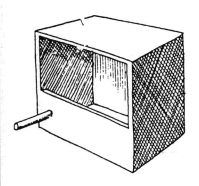

A nest box with a half-open front.

Grassfinches

The grassfinches are among the most popular of all finches as avicultural subjects. They inhabit Australasia and Malaysia and are primarily found in Australia. Most of them are brightly colored and many breed well in confinement. None have an eclipse plumage. Many are unique in drinking in the manner of pigeons, i.e., by sucking up the water and swallowing it without lifting their head.

In the natural state, these finches frequent grasslands and brushland areas and live in small flocks. The courtship display is fairly simple. The cock sits still with his flank feathers puffed out, his neck extended vertically and his bill pointing downward. During this time he sings a sort of melody with great effort and raises his body up and down with a twisting motion. In some species, the cock holds a blade of grass in his bill during the display. The nests are typical spherical structures, and the nestling birds show luminous mouth markings similar to those in the waxbills. The young are quite easy to rear since they feed mainly on seeds and green food which they eat themselves. Milk-soaked bread is a useful addition to the diet when young are in the nest. Some species will take insects.

All grassfinches are sociable and quite peaceful in mixed groups, although many will breed better if kept in single pairs. Some of the hens are subject to egg-binding, and it is therefore wise to allow them to breed only in fairly warm weather; they should be well supplied with cuttlebone.

Like other members of the finch family, the grassfinches usually appreciate nest boxes in which to sleep.

DIAMOND SPARROW

The Diamond Sparrow (*Emblema guttata*) comes from eastern Australia. Its upper parts are brownish gray; the forehead, head, and nape are light gray; the rump and upper tail coverts, bright red; underparts, snowy-white; a black band extends across the breast and down each side where it is heavily spotted with white. Tail, black; bill, red; legs and feet, gray. Length, 5 inches. The sexes are alike in coloration.

This lovely bird is easily kept but is one of the most difficult of Australian finches to breed in captivity. About the only method of determining sex in these birds is by the song and courting dance of the male. Young birds are mostly gray in color with a white breast and underparts, and show the red rump from the first; their bill is dull gray.

Along with the usual seed diet, Diamond Sparrows require a plentiful supply of insect food, thereby differing from most other grassfinches.

STAR FINCH

The Red-tailed or Star Finch (*Poephila ruficaudada*) comes from northern and eastern Australia. It is olive-green above, with the forehead, cheeks, and throat bright red, finely spotted white on the cheeks. The breast and sides are olive-gray, heavily spotted with white, and the center of the abdomen is yellow. Tail, red; bill, red. The female is lighter in color and shows less red on the face.

This species is hardy when acclimatized and breeds quite freely. The parents should be supplied with mealworms when rearing young. Immature birds are dull olive-green in color and show no red until about three months of age. They come into full color in about six months.

ZEBRA FINCH

Undoubtedly the most common of all finches in captivity is the little Zebra Finch (*Poephila guttata castanotis*), which is found throughout Australia generally. The upper parts are ash-gray, brownish on the wings. Tail is black with white bars. The cheeks are bright chestnut, with a white mark surrounded by black below and in front of the eye. Throat and upper breast are grayish white, barred with black, and separated from the white underparts by a heavy black band. Flanks, bright chestnut spotted with

white; bill, orange; legs and feet, salmon. Length, 4 inches. The female is gray above and buff below and lacks all the bright markings.

Several color variations of this bird have been produced in captivity and color standards have been established for these domestic forms. In addition to the normal (gray), there is a pure white form which retains the orange-red bill and legs; a silver form (dilute normal) which retains all of the markings but in very pale color; and the fawn Zebra Finch which also retains all of the characteristic markings but is fawn rather than gray in color. Pale forms of the latter are known as "creams" (actually "dilute fawns"). There are also pied and "marked" forms.

All are easily bred in small nest boxes. No more nesting material than is absolutely necessary should be given, as the birds will often spend all of their time building nests. The cocks are quite pugnacious toward other birds when breeding. No special food is required for the young. The young birds leave the nest after about 16 days and are gray all over with black bills. When they are ten to 12 weeks of age, their bills turn red and the males start to acquire their colored markings.

Being entirely domesticated, they are very prolific and will breed the year around if allowed to do so. It is best to take no more than two or three clutches from them during the course of a year.

Shaft-tailed Grassfinch, *Poephila acuticauda*, also known as the Long-tailed Grassfinch. It is an attractive bird native to northern and northwestern Australia. Photo by T. Tilford.

SHAFT-TAILED FINCH

Although not brightly colored, the Shaft-tailed Finch (*Poephila acuticauda*) is one of the most attractive of the grassfinches. It comes from northern and northwestern Australia. The upper parts are rosy brown, darker on the wings; the crown and sides of the head are silvery gray. There is a large black bib on the throat, and the eyes are encircled by a black oval. Upper tail coverts and rump are white, with the latter crossed by a black band. Underparts, fawn; thighs, vent and underwing coverts, white. Tail, black, with the two central feathers elongated into two wires. Bill, yellow; legs and feet, red. Length, 6 inches. The sexes are alike.

HECK'S SHAFT-TAILED FINCH

There are actually two forms of this race of grassfinch known as Heck's Shaft-tailed Finch (*Poephila acuticauda hecki*), one of which has a bright red bill. Both forms are very free breeders in captivity, being among the most prolific of all the grassfinches, with the possible exception of the Zebra Finch. They can be quite quarrelsome when breeding, and pairs are best kept in an aviary by themselves. Four or five white eggs constitute a clutch, and both birds incubate for a period of about 14 days. Young birds are more or less gray all over, paler underneath. Adult males usually have a somewhat larger bib on the throat than adult females.

GOULDIAN FINCH

The most beautifully colored grassfinch and, indeed, one of the most beautiful of all birds, is the lovely Gouldian Finch (*Poephila gouldiae*) from Queensland and northern and northwestern Australia. The back and wings are grass-green; the forehead, crown and throat are red, surrounded by a line of black that in turn is followed by a wider line of bright turquoise blue that widens at the nape. The rump is light blue; the breast, deep purple; upper abdomen, orange; lower abdomen, yellow fading to white. Tail, black with the two central feathers longer than the others and pointed on the ends; bill, white with a red tip; legs and feet, pinkish. Length, 4.5 inches. The female is similar but duller in color.

This bird is also seen (more commonly) with black on the head in place of the red, or (rarely) with orange-yellow in the same area. It is a somewhat difficult subject in captivity in certain respects, sometimes dropping dead for no apparent reason at all. If good stock is obtained, however, it is not too difficult to breed. No insectivore or live food is required, and young are reared on seeds and green food exclusively.

Gouldians do not readily change their breeding season to conform with the Northern Hemisphere and usually go to nest sometime around July. Since they are not very hardy in regards to temperature—and hens are subject to egg-binding—it is difficult to keep them in open outdoor aviaries in the colder climates.

Incubation lasts for 12 or 13 days, and the young birds when hatched are greenish gray above and yellowish gray below; they do not show any of the color pattern found on the adults. Adult plumage is not attained until six to 12 months of age. They are aggressive towards other birds.

RED-HEADED PARROT FINCH

Another very beautiful grassfinch is the Red-headed Parrot Finch (*Erythrura psittacea*), which comes from New Caledonia. It is bright glossy green in color, with the head, throat and upper breast, bright red. The rump and tail are also red. The bill is black; legs and feet, gray. Length, 4.5 inches. The sexes are alike, although females sometimes show less red on the face.

This species is not common in captivity, but is quite easily kept and bred. In its native Pacific island habitat it places its nests in holes in rocks and breeds in small colonies. The male builds the nest and helps in incubation, which extends for a period of about 14 days. The young leave the nest around 21 days after hatching, at which time they are dull green in color and have a dull red tail. Some show a little red on the face but this varies with individuals. The lower mandible of the beak is bright yellow and gradually changes to black. Full adult color is achieved by about four months. Parrot Finches do not do well in small cages.

MANNIKINS

The mannikins or nuns are the least colorful members of this family. They inhabit Africa, Asia, Malaysia and Australasia but are most numerous in the Malaysia and New Guinea regions.

Most of them live in large flocks and frequent reed beds and grasslands. They have short, thick beaks and their food consists almost wholly of vegetable matter (seeds and greens), although some of the African forms eat a considerable amount of insects.

The cocks perform a courtship dance resembling that of the grassfinches. Most of these birds are difficult to breed in captivity, although there are some that do so quite freely.

Nestlings show the luminous mouth markings characteristic of this family, but the pattern is unique to this group. The palate is marked with horseshoe-like dark lines or blotches and the gape has a swollen line, but shows no warts or lobes.

Some of these birds are quarrelsome and dangerous to smaller and weaker birds. Most are very hardy and live for many years in confinement.

JAVA RICE BIRD

A very popular finch, the Java Sparrow or Rice Bird (*Padda oryzivora*) comes originally from Java and Bali but is now also found throughout Malaysia. It is fairly large (5.5 inches) and mainly a beautiful slate-gray in color, with a black head

Above: Cluster of four Society Finches, *Lonchura striata.* Society Finches are also called Bengalese. The Society Finch is an entirely domestic form, believably cultivated by Chinese and Japanese breeders many centuries ago. Photo by R. and V. Moat. Facing page: Queen Whydah, *Vidua regia*, demonstrates the long beautiful tail that is characteristic of some of the whydahs, including the Paradise Whydah. Photo by H. Schrempp.

and white cheeks. The abdomen is pinkish fading to white underneath, and the wing flights and tail feathers are black. The bill is very large and bright pink in color. Legs and feet, reddish. Sexes alike, but the female's beak is somewhat smaller at the base than that of the male. A pure white form (with red bill and legs) has been produced in captivity.

The Java Sparrow makes an excellent cage or aviary bird but is inclined to bully smaller finches. It makes an excellent pet if taken from the nest and hand-reared. Its diet should contain "paddy" or unhulled rice.

Imported wild-caught specimens are not easily bred, although the pure white form breeds readily. The period of incubation is about 14 days. Not all young birds in the nest of a white Java will necessarily be white, some may be gray in color and others may be partly white. The gray ones will never be anything but duplicates of the original gray bird but some of those showing whitish feathers may molt out all white, while others will end up mottled. These mottled birds are known as calico Java Rice Birds.

The normal young Java is gray all over, darker on the head, and lacks the white cheek patches. Its beak is dark brown and the full adult plumage with a red beak is not assumed until about the age of five months. Java Sparrows are sometimes sold under the name "Java Temple Birds."

RIBBON FINCH

The Cut-throat or Ribbon Finch (*Amadina fasciata*) comes from Africa. The general color is brown, darker on the wings, each feather edged with black and showing white spots on the sides of the abdomen. A bright red collar extends across the throat from ear to ear. Bill, yellowish white. The female is similar but lacks the crimson collar.

This species is somewhat inclined to bully smaller and weaker birds. It is quite readily bred in confinement in either cage or aviary, and its eggs hatch in about 12 days. The young leave the nest after 21 days. Young males resemble their mother and do not acquire the crimson throat collar until their first molt.

BRONZE MANNIKIN

The very tiny (3-inch) Bronze Mannikin (*Lonchura cucullata*) is found throughout tropical Africa. The crown, sides of head and throat are black; the head is glossed with green. The upper parts, including wings, are gray-brown, with bronze-black spots on the shoulder. Rump and upper tail coverts possess irregular black and grayish markings. Tail, black; flanks and abdomen, white, streaked and barred with wavy black lines. The female is similar but slightly duller in color.

This species will breed in captivity. The young birds are quite different in appearance from their parents. They show no black but are reddish brown all over with darker wings and tail.

SOCIETY FINCH

One of the most interesting of all the small mannikins is the Society Finch or Bengalese. This is an entirely domestic form, the ancestors of which are not definitely known. It was produced over a period of many centuries by Chinese and Japanese breeders and comes in three color varieties: pure white, chocolate and white, and fawn and white. Tri-colored and crested forms as well as selfs (solid colors) are also sometimes seen. The dark markings are never found on the same areas of the body in two different birds. The sexes are exactly alike in appearance and may only be distinguished by the male's little song with which he constantly serenades his mate. It is possible to distinguish the sexes by listening to the calls of two birds that are separated and out of sight of each other: the male's call is a single syllable note that the female will answer with a three or four syllable call.

The Society Finch is one of the most easily bred of all cage birds, breeding equally well in cage or aviary, and is often used as a foster parent for the young of other species of finch, as they will even incubate and rear the young of birds considerably larger than themselves; however, they will not feed any food other than seeds and greens, which makes them of no use in rearing such birds as waxbills.

Society Finches should be given nest boxes for breeding and kept one pair to an enclosure because, although they do not quarrel, they all crowd into the same nest box to sleep, making it impossible for any one hen to incubate eggs. Young birds resemble their parents but have shorter tails.

NUTMEG MANNIKIN

The Spice or Nutmeg Mannikin (*Lonchura punctulata*) has a wide distribution throughout India, Ceylon, southern Asia, Malaysia, etc. It is chocolate-brown above, darker on the head, with narrow light shaft streaks. Face and throat, deep chestnut. The abdomen is whitish buff; the breasts and sides, spotted white over brown. The tail is washed with yellow. Bill, bluish black; legs, gray. Length, 4 inches. The sexes are alike.

This species is not too difficult to breed if a true pair can be obtained. Spice Mannikins live well on seeds and greens alone, seldom touching insect food, although this food should be offered to them.

Bird dealers in India have been known to dye this bird different colors (usually green) and offer them as "painted finches!"

CHESTNUT MANNIKIN

The Black-hooded Nun or Chestnut Mannikin (*Lonchura malacca*) ranges from the Himalayas through Indo-China. It is entirely deep chestnut in color with a black head, neck and abdomen. The bill is silvery gray. Length, 4 inches. The sexes are alike.

Above: Chestnut-breasted Finch, *Lonchura castaneothorax*, sports a very attractively colored plumage, but it is not commonly kept in the fancy. Photo by R. and V. Moat. Facing page: Chestnut Mannikin, *Lonchura malacca*. Photo by T. Tilford.

This bird seldom breeds in captivity but at one time was one of the most commonly imported of the so-called nuns. Its toenails (like those of the related forms) seem to grow much too fast, and it is usually necessary to catch the birds regularly and trim their claws to prevent injuries and accidents related to overgrown claws. Of course, if you are inexperienced in this practice, you must seek assistance.

Young birds are pale brown all over; traces of black start to appear about four to five weeks after the young leave the nest.

THREE-COLORED NUN

The race known as the Three-colored Nun (*Lonchura ferruginosa malacca*) comes originally from India and Ceylon. It is chestnut-brown in color, with the head and upper breast black. The lower breast and sides are pure white, and the middle of the abdomen and underparts are black. The bill is silver-gray. The sexes are alike.

This form has been bred in captivity on several occasions. They incubate for about 14 days, and the young leave the nest about 23 days later. All of these nuns like to sleep in nest boxes at night.

Weavers & Whydahs

The weaverbirds (family Ploceidae) are a large group (156 species) of small seed-eating birds that resemble the typical finches in appearance. They are found mainly in Africa, but also inhabit Europe and Asia in some numbers. Their name comes from the elaborate and skillfully woven nests that they construct.

Most of the species are quite hardy and may be kept in outdoor aviaries the year around once acclimatized. All of them may be fed on millet, canary and other small grass seeds with some soft food (insectivore mixture), as well as greens and fruit. They are also fond of mealworms. Keep grit, fresh water, and cuttlebone available.

ORANGE WEAVER

The most common and best known form is the Orange Weaver or Bishop (*Euplectes orix franciscana*) of northeastern and western Africa. The male in breeding plumage is deep velvety black, with the neck, chin, breast, back and elongated tail coverts, orange-red. The wings are tawny with dark brown stripes. Bill and legs, grayish flesh colored. Length, 4.5 inches. The older these birds are, the darker the orange-red becomes. When displaying, the feathers of the neck stand out and form a ruff. The female is light brown with dark streaks. As with most others of this group, it is very difficult to pick a pair when the male is out of color. It is rarely bred in captivity.

GOLDEN-CROWNED BISHOP

The most common of the yellow and black weavers is the Napoleon or Golden-crowned Bishop (*Euplectes afra*) from western Africa. The male in color is bright golden yellow with a velvety black face, chin, lower breast and abdomen. Wings and tail are brownish. Bill, black; legs, flesh colored. Length, 4 inches. The female is light brown, marked and streaked with darker brown, and her face and breast are somewhat yellowish. The male resembles her when out of color.

This species has often bred in captivity, laying three or four white eggs, lightly speckled with brownish black; incubation lasts about 13 or 14 days.

The whydahs or widow birds are closely related to the weavers but are easily distinguished by their habit of scratching up the ground with their feet in the manner of game birds. Like the weaver cocks, whydah males go out of color for part of the year.

They are parasitic nesters, and commonly deposit their eggs in the nests of certain waxbills. All are good aviary subjects and easily kept but are not easily bred in captivity because of their odd nesting habits. As with the typical weavers, they do not attain full adult plumage until their second year. The cocks are polygamous.

PIN-TAILED WHYDAH

One of the most common of the long-tailed forms is the Pin-tailed Whydah or Widow Bird (*Vidua macroura*) found throughout tropical Africa. When in color the male is glossy black above; the underparts, sides of the head, lower back, and a stripe across the wings are white. The long (9-inch) tail feathers are black and very narrow. Bill and legs red. Length (including the tail), 13 inches. The female is tawny, speckled with black. This species is very quarrelsome.

PARADISE WHYDAH

The best known and most popular whydah is the Paradise Whydah or Widow Bird (*Vidua paradisaea aucupum*) from Senegal and western Africa. The male when in color is black with a very wide reddish brown collar around the neck and yellowish white underparts. His tail has the two center feathers long (11 inches) and plume-like; the two outer feathers shorter, wide at the base and narrowing to long curled wire-like ends. Beak, black; legs flesh colored. The female (and the male in eclipse) is reddish gray streaked with black. This is a very beautiful bird when in breeding plumage, is easily kept, and will not bother any other birds.

Bibliography

FINCHES AND SOFT-BILLED BIRDS
By Henry Bates and Robert Busenbark
ISBN 0-86622-654-0
TFH H-908
Audience: The classic reference work. The most complete book on seed-eating, soft-billed birds (as opposed to "hard-billed" or parrot-like birds). Every important cage bird is discussed and illustrated in color. A must-have for every keeper of these birds.
Hard cover, 5½ x 8½", 735 pages
159 black and white photos, 246 color photos

FINCHES AND THEIR CARE
By Carl Aschenborn
ISBN 0-86622-959-0
TS-107
Audience: There are more than 200 full-color photos of both popular and rare finch species in this book, perfectly complementing the sensible advice the author provides about every topic of concern to finch fanciers, especially beginners.
Hardcover, 8½ x 11", 160 pages

BIRD DISEASES: An Introduction To The Study Of Birds In Health And Disease
By Drs. L. Arnall and I.F. Keymer
ISBN 0-87666-950-X
TFH H-964
Audience: Highly specialized book. Written for bird pathologists and bird dealers. It requires a thorough education in biology to be understood, but experienced bird lovers can recognize symptoms and diseases from the many illustrations and thus be able to treat their own birds since "bird doctors" are so few and far between.
Hard cover, 6 x 9", 528 pages
304 black and white photos, 99 color photos